Discover India
State by State

OFF TO MANIPUR

SONIA MEHTA

PUFFIN BOOKS

An imprint of Penguin Random House

PUFFIN BOOKS

USA | Canada | UK | Ireland | Australia
New Zealand | India | South Africa | China | Singapore

Puffin Books is part of the Penguin Random House group of companies whose addresses can be found at global.penguinrandomhouse.com

Published by Penguin Random House India Pvt. Ltd
4th Floor, Capital Tower 1, MG Road,
Gurugram 122 002, Haryana, India

First published in Puffin Books by Penguin Random House India 2018

Text, design and illustrations copyright © Quadrum Solutions Pvt. Ltd 2018
Series copyright © Penguin Random House India 2018

Picture Credits
P 10: Kangla Fort, Imphal (© Meghroddur [CC BY-SA 4.0 (https://creativecommons.org/licenses/by-sa/4.0)], from Wikimedia Commons), Kakching (© Anil09400622469 [CC BY-SA 4.0 (https://creativecommons.org/licenses/by-sa/4.0)], from Wikimedia Commons); P 30: Uttra Sanglen, Kangla Fort (© Mashalti [CC BY-SA 3.0 (https://creativecommons.org/licenses/by-sa/3.0)], from Wikimedia Commons); P 36: Khongjom War Memorial (© Diamond Oina [CC BY-SA 3.0 (https://creativecommons.org/licenses/by-sa/3.0)], from Wikimedia Commons); P 46: Singju (© Punshiba18 [GFDL (http://www.gnu.org/copyleft/fdl.html) or CC BY-SA 3.0 (https://creativecommons.org/licenses/by-sa/3.0)], via Wikimedia Commons); P 47: Chahou Kheer (©By BengaliHindu [CC BY-SA 4.0 (https://creativecommons.org/licenses/by-sa/4.0)], from Wikimedia Commons); P 49: Ras lila performers (© Punshiba18 [CC BY-SA 3.0 (https://creativecommons.org/licenses/by-sa/3.0)], from Wikimedia Commons)

The views and opinions expressed in this book are the author's own and the facts are as reported by her, which have been verified to the extent possible, and the publishers are not in any way liable for the same.

The information in this book is based on research from bonafide sites and published books and is true to the best of the author's knowledge at the time of going to print. The author is not responsible for any further changes or developments occurring post the publication of this book. This series is not a comprehensive representation of the states of India but is intended to give children a flavour of the lifestyles and cultures of different states. All illustrations are artistic representations only.

ISBN 9780143440956

Design and layout by Quadrum Solutions Pvt. Ltd

Printed at Repro India Limited

www.penguin.co.in

Hello Kids!

I'm so happy you are reading this book. India is an incredible country and there are lots of things about it that we never get to hear about.

I discovered India because my father was in the Indian army. He was posted to many places all over India—and we dutifully followed him. Can you imagine that by the time I was in the tenth standard, I had changed nine schools? Of course it was hard making new friends almost every year, but the good part was that I got to live in so many places. Right from Kerala, where I was born, to Kashmir, Jhansi, Shillong, Chandigarh, Goa . . . the list is long.

Every time I go to a new place, I feel amazed at how different each state is from the other—and yet, how similar. Did you know that we can see monuments from the Stone Age right here in India? Or that we have more than twenty official languages, and most Indians know three or four on an average? Or even that some of the world's most amazing scientific marvels were invented in India?

Oh, there are many, many, many fun and fantastic things about the states of India, which we simply must get to know.

So get your backpack ready, get set to meet some new friends and join me on a fun trip as we **DISCOVER INDIA, STATE BY STATE**.

I hope you enjoy reading this book as much as I have enjoyed writing it. I would love to hear from you. So do write to me at sonia.mehta@quadrumltd.com.

Lots of love,
Sonia Aunty

Mishki and Pushka have come to visit Earth from their home planet, Zoomba. They have never seen such an amazing place. Zoomba doesn't have trees and mountains and rivers like Earth does. But the people look exactly the same. When they come to Earth, they meet a sweet old man whom they call Daadu Dolma. Daadu Dolma shows them all the wonderful places in India and tells Mishki and Pushka all about them.

Mishki and Pushka can't believe what they see. They have seen a lot of Earth, but they have never, ever seen a place like India.

They are off to explore India state by state :)

Mishki

Mishki is a curious little girl. She is always asking loads of questions. On her home planet, she is always getting into trouble for poking her nose into things that are not her business.

Pushka

Pushka is Mishki's brother. He loves adventure. He is always ready for a new challenge. Whether it's climbing a mountain, or diving into a cold, cold sea, he is up for it.

Daadu Dolma

Daadu Dolma is a wise old man who has lived on Earth longer than the mountains and the seas. No one knows quite how old he is, but he certainly has been around. He knows everything about everything.

Mishki is awake extra early. She has packed her bags and is longing to set off on another trip with Daadu Dolma and Pushka.

'Wake up, Pushka,' she says, shaking him hard.

Pushka sits up and rubs his eyes.

'Oh, is it time to go already?' he asks sleepily.

'Yes, it is,' Daadu replies. 'I hope you two have packed some warm clothes. The place we're going to visit can get cold.'

'But where are we going?' demands Pushka. 'I hope it's somewhere I can eat some good food.'

'That's all you're interested in,' giggles Mishki. 'Daadu, I know we are going to Manipur. So what are we going to see there?'

'You'll see lovely mountains, learn about the state's fascinating history and meet some wonderful people,' Daadu answers. 'Let's get going.'

Mishki and Pushka pick up their bags. They are

OFF TO MANIPUR!!!

A SNEAK PEEK

LAND AHOY!
About the land, water, rivers, mountains and seas.
page 6

LONG, LONG AGO
The story of the state.
page 12

TALK TIME
What language do the people speak?
page 20

BRICKS AND STONES
Of houses, buildings and bridges.
page 28

A PEEP INTO THEIR LIFE
The music, dance and lifestyle of the people.
page 22

STANDING STRONG
Famous monuments in Manipur.
page 30

WORKING HARD
What work do people do?
page 40

YUM YUM YUM
Food, food, food. What's the yummy food of Manipur?
page 44

AUTOGRAPH, PLEASE?
Famous people—past and present.
page 50

WHAT TO WEAR?
The clothes they wear.
page 48

ONCE UPON A TIME . . .
Stories from the state.
page 54

Land ahoy!

Which part of India is Manipur in, Daadu?

Manipur is in the north-east of India. It's one of the seven states that are called the Seven Sisters.

HILLY NEIGHBOURS

Manipur has some hilly neighbours with whom it shares a lot—its history, its culture and its food habits among other things. It is surrounded by the Indian states of Nagaland, Assam and Mizoram, and the country of Myanmar (once known as Burma).

Manipur means 'the land of gems'.

ON THE MAP

To see exactly where **Manipur** is on the map of India, go to

http://www.mapsofindia.com/maps/india/india-political-map.htm

GENTLE SLOPES

The great Himalayas begin to gently slope downwards as they go south. It is on these slopes that Manipur sits. You could say it has two main regions. One is the Manipur river valley and the other is a spread of mountainous land. This land has all the beauty of the Himalayas without the harsh climate.

WATER, WATER EVERYWHERE

When you hear 'Manipur', you think of Loktak Lake. This spectacular lake is enormous and is where Manipur's most important river is born— the Manipur river. This river flows southwards, joining another river called the Myittha. Other rivers that flow around and through this lovely state are the Chindwin, the Surma and the Barak.

Loktak Lake

COOL, COLD, COLDER

In the valleys, the people of Manipur enjoy the cool and pleasant weather. But as you climb higher, it gets colder and colder. During winter, it can get cold! There's plenty of rain too, which is good for farmers but not so great if you want to go for a walk.

Shirui Hills

HILLY BILLY

There are plenty of hills in Manipur. They are connected to each other by ridges and spurs. The main hills are the Naga Hills, the East Manipur Hills, the Mizo Hills, the Chin Hills, the Shirui Hills and the West Manipur Hills.

Wow! Look at all those shades of green!

GO GREEN

Rhododendron

The hills of Manipur are full of dense forests, with trees that are very useful to people. Bamboo and teak are the main trees found here, and people make lots of things with them. The forests also have magnificent oak, magnolia and pine trees. You can also see some lovely flowers, like rhododendrons, poppies and primroses.

AWESOME ANIMALS

The abundance of trees and forests here means that there are loads of animals. Manipur is proud of its wonderful wildlife, like the magnificent Asiatic elephant, the spotted leopard and the wild buffalo. If you're lucky, you might see the famous Indian one-horned rhinoceros, which is a highly endangered species. You might also see a *gaur* (the world's largest wild bison) and the brow-antlered deer, among other incredible creatures.

FUN FACTS

State animal
Brow-antlered deer

State tree
Uningthou

State bird
Mrs Hume's Pheasant

State flower
Siroi lily

HIDDEN WORDS

The rhododendron is a lovely flower you see in Manipur. Can you make ten smaller words from this word?

RHODODENDRON

_____ _____ _____ _____

_____ _____ _____ _____

CITY CITY BANG BANG

Manipur has some lovely little cities and charming towns.

IMPHAL

Believed to be one of India's most ancient cities, Imphal is Manipur's capital. It is home to the Kangla Fort and is known for its wonderful scenery. It gets its name from the Manipuri word *yumphal*, meaning 'land of many villages'. It is believed that the game of polo originated here.

BISHNUPUR

This town gets its name from the ancient temple of Lord Vishnu—its star attraction. It was also the place where a lot of fighting took place between the Japanese and the Allied Forces during World War II. Many descendants of the Japanese soldiers who lost their lives here visit this town to pay homage to their heroes and ancestors.

KAKCHING

Kakching is famous for being the town from where Netaji Subhas Chandra Bose took his last flight, before it controversially crashed. Today, this town serves as an important base for the Indian Army.

JIRIBAM

This town is called 'the western gate of Manipur'. Said to be one of the state's fastest growing towns, it has a wonderful potpourri of different communities and tribes.

MOREH

Sitting on the border of India and Myanmar, Moreh is home to many different tribes. It's an important town for trade between India and Myanmar and is fast becoming Manipur's commercial capital.

Jiribam is famous for its tea estates

MOIRANG

Historically, the town of Moirang is best known for the ancient temple of Lord Thangjing, a very ancient deity. It is also believed that this is where the legendary love story of Khamba–Thoibi took place (we'll learn more about this later). Moirang is located very close to the famous Loktak Lake.

Long, long ago

SO MANY KINGS, SO MANY NAMES

History says that Manipur has been ruled by hundreds of kings over hundreds of years. Its ancient history actually goes back to 33 CE. Through the ages, Manipur has had many names. Here are some of them.

Sanna Leipak

Tilli Koktong

Poirei Lam

Mitei Lipak

Meitrabak

Daadu, I am confused. If Manipur is called one of the Seven Sisters, is its history very different from the rest of India's?

In many ways, it is different. In fact, the history of Manipur is quite old. Come, let's have a look.

AT FIRST

The first famous king of Manipur was a ruler called Pakhangba. He was believed to be the first proper king of Manipur. It was during his time that the Meitei culture began to come to life. He brought together different tribes under his rule, establishing the kingdom of Kangla.

King Pakhangba was named after an ancient Meitei deity called Pakhangba, who is represented by the image of a dragon.

A game called sagol kangjei is played here, and the chiefs of different tribes used to enjoy playing too. People say that the now well-known sport of polo originated from this game.

THE GROWTH OF THE MEITEI

After Pakhangba, his heirs ruled for many years. But eventually the tribes started fighting amongst each other. Finally, a tribe called the Meiteis or the Ningthoujas prevailed over the rest. For the next several hundred years, the Meiteis grew, establishing their supremacy over the other tribes.

SPOT THE DIFFERENCES

Can you believe that polo is said to have originated in Manipur? Spot ten differences in these two pictures of a modern polo player.

THE GREAT LAW GIVER

A king called Loiyamba Shinyen ruled this region for a while. His reign was important because he introduced many new administrative systems that made his kingdom very organized. These systems lasted for many hundreds of years. He was called the Great Law Giver.

THE KINGDOM OF KANGLEIPAK

Another king called Loiyamba established the kingdom of Kangleipak. He was known to be the first ruler who wrote a proper constitution for his kingdom, with very detailed rules and laws.

CHINESE INVADERS

Chinese invaders always had an eye on the lovely land of Manipur. They hoped to expand their kingdom. A king called Meidingu Khagemba of the Kangleipak Dynasty defeated them. He expanded his kingdom into parts of what is now Myanmar. He was a wise ruler and introduced metal currency. He also supported literature. His reign was known as the golden age of Meitei literature.

WHAT'S IN A NAME?

It was in the 1700s, during the rule of a king from the Naga tribe called Meidingu Pamheiba, that Hinduism became the state religion. The Sanskrit name Manipur first appeared during this time. Meidingu Pamheiba called himself Gharib Nawaz. For a while after his death, Manipur became a part of the kingdom of Burma.

RHYME TIME

Mishki is writing an essay about the kingdom of Manipur. She wants to find five words that mean 'king'. Can you circle the words for her?

Czar

Rajah

Lieutenant

Monarch

Soldier

Captain

Ruler

Major

Leader

Manager

Sovereign

Colonel

THE BURMESE INVADE

The Manipuri king Jai Singh (also known as Ching-Thang Khomba) appealed to the British, who had by this time colonized India. He asked for their help in getting rid of the Burmese. For the next several years, the British and Manipuri rulers were allies. The Burmese would invade Manipur frequently, trying their best to capture the territory. These have been documented in history as the Burmese invasions.

PROTECTED BY THE BRITISH

The subsequent king of Manipur, Gambhir Singh (also called Chinglen Nongdrenkhomba), continued to receive help from the British who sent sepoys and ammunition and even trained Manipuri troops. Finally, the Burmese were defeated. For many years, Manipur remained peaceful.

Nara Singh

Gambhir Singh

INTERNAL SKIRMISHES

Many kings ruled after Gambhir Singh. One of them—Nara Singh—grabbed the throne and held on to it till he died. But sadly, after his death, many members of his family fought for the throne, and there were many struggles and rebellions.

THE BRITISH TAKE CHARGE

The British decided to recognize one of the heirs to the throne, Juvraj Kulachandra Singh, as the new king. They sent troops to capture one of the main people behind the rebellion—a prince called Tikendrajit. There was a lot of fighting. Kulachandra Singh was put into jail. Many people lost their lives. This terrible event was called the Manipur Expedition. For many years, this area was full of violence and turbulence.

The battles of those days were so fierce. Those soldiers must have been really gutsy!

CRACK THE CODE

Mishki is saying something in code. Can you crack the code and figure out what she is saying?

S = 1	H = 2	I = 3	O = 4	R = 5	T = 6	Y = 7

A = 8	F = 9	C = 10	G = 11	N = 12

2 3 1 6 4 5 7   3 1

_ _ _ _ _ _ _   _ _

9 8 1 10 3 12 8 6 3 12 11

_ _ _ _ _ _ _ _ _ _ _

THE JAPANESE CONNECTION

While all this action was taking place in Manipur, the Japanese had sent an army to occupy most of the neighbouring areas, as well as a part of Manipur. World War II ensued soon after.

A CHILD RULER

A five-year-old child called Meidingngu Churachand was made the ruler for some time, and the British briefly allowed Manipur to be independent while they concentrated on the rest of the country. The little boy grew up and ruled his kingdom for a few years.

Subhas Chandra Bose tried to ally with the Japanese in an attempt to get rid of the British. He established the Indian National Army, a breakaway unit from the British-controlled Indian Army, which fought against the British along with the Japanese.

WORLD WAR II

It seemed as if the whole world was in turmoil during World War II. To fight British troops, the Japanese bombed Manipur, which was under the British. The British and Indian forces together quelled the Japanese attacks. Unfortunately, there were many casualties.

Japanese soldiers during World War II

AN INDEPENDENT INDIA

Things were taking place in the rest of India as well. There were riots and protests demanding that the British leave India for good. And finally, in 1947, they did. India became independent and Manipur became a princely state, which was a part of the Indian government. A king called Maharaja Bodhchandra was the last king of Manipur. After several years of India's independence, Manipur was finally declared a proper state in 1972.

That's quite a turbulent history!

WHAT'S ODD?

There's something odd in each row. Can you help Pushka circle it?

KING	MONARCH	RULER	STUDENT

TROOPS	SOLDIERS	TEACHERS	BATTALION

JAPANESE	PRIESTS	BRITISH	INDIAN

MANY TRIBES, MANY DIALECTS

As we've seen, there have been many tribes who have lived in Manipur for centuries. So there are many languages and dialects spoken in this state. One of the main languages is Manipuri, called Meiteilon or Meitei by the local people. It is from the Tibetan–Burmese language family.

Some Meitei Phrases

I do not understand =
Ei bhab taade
Please =
Chaanbeeduna
I Love Manipur =
Ei Manipur nungshi

Yes = Hoi
No = Natte
Thank you =
Thaagatchari

Hello =
Khurumjari
Goodbye =
Chatcharage

How are you? =
Nung ngai
biribra adombo?
Fine =
Nungaijari

Tangkhul,
Kuki, Lushai, Hmar, Paite
and Thadou are some of
the other languages
spoken in
Manipur.

Manipur is
beautiful =
Manipur phajei
Congratulations
= Thakatchari

Welcome =
Lengsinbirakoo

WORD MATCH

Pushka is trying his best to remember the new words he's learnt. Can you help him by matching the English words to their Manipuri phrases?

| I love Manipur | Goodbye | Hello | Congratulations | Please |

| Chatcharage | Thakatchari | Chaanbeeduna | Khurumjari | Ei Manipur nungshi |

A peep into their life

The people living here seem to be so cheerful, and their culture is really interesting. I'm sure they have some amazing festivals too.

That's quite true. Since this state has many tribes and is so close to the border, there are many different cultures that have mixed together to create Manipur's unique culture.

GAME TIME

Here's an amazing fact: Manipur has an incredible culture of ancient games. Many of these have evolved into modern games that people play even today.

Kang

KANG SHANABA

Kang shanaba is a game played on a mud floor. The contestants have to hit a target with a *kang*, a flat, oblong object that used to be made of ivory. The game is played during the Manipuri new year, *Cheiraoba*. People here play this strictly during this period, for they believe that if played at odd times, they will get attacked by evil spirits. What a fun game!

MANIPURI POLO

Sagol kangjei is the original form of polo, a game which is played all over the world. During a game of sagol kangjei, each player has a polo stick made of bamboo. The players mount horses and chase the ball, aiming to hit it into the goal. It is said that the British, who are great horse lovers, were fascinated by the game and modified it, making it the international sport of polo.

THANG-TA AND SARIT SARAT

This is a Manipuri martial art that is centuries old. Originally it was a way for people to practise their battle skills. It's strenuous and requires a lot of hard practice. There are many rituals and rules that participants have to strictly follow.

BOAT RACE

The Meiteis believe that by worshipping their boats (called *hiyang hiren*), evil spirits are kept away. They pray to their boats and have an annual boat race called *Hiyang Tannaba*. The rowers wear dramatic headgear and stunning costumes. People also have these races when there is a major calamity, like a flood or an earthquake.

23

DANCE DANCE

There are many fun dances that the tribes of Manipur enjoy. Let's find out more about some of them.

RAS LILA

When you think of Manipur, you might picture dancers doing the typical Manipuri dance, also called *Ras Lila*. This dance symbolizes the eternal love between Radha and Krishna. It is performed in temple courtyards through the night, while devotees watch in rapt attention. The costume is dramatic. Women wear stiff, barrel-shaped skirts called *poloi*. Men wear bright and coloured dhotis called *dhoras* that cover their bodies from the waist down.

DANCING TO MEET ANCESTORS

The *Maibi* dance is one through which the Meitei believe they can connect with their ancestors. Every year, during a festival called *Lai Haraoba*, they perform this dance, in which they relive the past, right from the time the world was created.

THE DANCE OF THE DRUM

Pung cholom is a dance in which the star is the instrument—the drum (*pung*). Some of the performers play the instrument, making the sound go from a soft whisper to a dramatic climax, while the others dance to the pulsating rhythm.

It's hard to just sit and watch. You feel like dancing along!

Poloi

A LOVE STORY

The Khamba–Thoibi dance is a lovely dance duet, with male and female dancers depicting the legendary love story of Khamba and Thoibi, two star-crossed lovers. People believe that the two lovers performed this dance in front of an idol of Lord Thangjing. Even now, people perform this dance for the same deity.

HANDY HANDICRAFT

Manipur's handicrafts are known around the world. The talented craftspeople here weave cloth and bamboo and chisel wood to make wonderful objects.

WEAVING WONDERS

It is said by some that a goddess called Chitnu Tamitnu discovered cotton and produced a magical yarn. Another belief is that yet another goddess, Panthoibi, spotted a spider producing the thread and using it make a fine web. Some say it was she who started the ancient tradition of weaving. Today most of the weavers in Manipur are women. Tribal shawls with intricate patterns are typical of this state.

BAMBOO BONANZA

The abundance of bamboo forests here makes it easy for people to get plenty of bamboo. Making bamboo baskets has been a tradition in Manipur for centuries. Weavers make special baskets for ceremonies, for domestic use and even to use as fishing equipment.

PERFECT POTTERY

The culture of pottery is very old. Different tribes specialize in different styles and patterns of pottery, usually in red, maroon and black colours. They make pots for rituals and ceremonies, but now these pots are used as decorative items across India.

Go ahead! Try this word search! It'll be fun.

WORD SEARCH

Some words related to Manipuri culture are hidden in this word grid. Can you find them all?

| Kang | Hiyang Tannaba | Polo | Sarit Sarat | Maibi | Lai Haraoba | Pung Cholom | Cheiraoba |

H	I	Y	A	N	G	T	A	N	N	A	B	A
A	D	F	H	O	I	U	Y	T	E	R	W	Q
Z	X	P	U	N	G	C	H	O	L	O	M	N
L	A	I	H	A	R	A	O	B	A	C	V	B
D	S	A	I	U	I	Y	T	R	E	W	Q	M
F	G	S	A	R	I	T	S	A	R	A	T	X
H	J	K	L	Z	X	C	V	B	N	M	Q	Z
W	N	M	M	A	I	B	I	Q	S	Q	W	X
P	O	L	O	H	B	V	X	K	A	N	G	Z
F	E	W	Q	C	H	E	I	R	A	O	B	A

Bricks and stones

I would love to see a Manipuri house, Daadu. Can we visit one?

I'll take you to see one. There are many types of houses because there are so many different tribes. But they all use similar materials—mostly natural.

TRIBAL ABODES

Most tribes build houses using cane, wood, bamboo and thatch—all materials easily available to them. There's usually a veranda, an enclosed space for animals and a kitchen area. The kitchen often has a fireplace, called *phunga meifam*, right in the centre of the room, above which meat and fish are hung out to dry.

MEITEI YUMJAO— A TYPICAL HOUSE

The Meiteis, said to be the largest tribe in Manipur, are very skilled craftspeople. They are also terrific architects. Their houses, called *yumjaos*, are perfect examples of Manipuri tribal houses.

ROOF TALES

The way the Meiteis build their roofs is exceptionally clever. They look like simple thatched roofs, but there's a non-flammable material between two layers of thatch that prevents it from catching fire.

Clever!

Yumjaos are truly eco-friendly. They are both economical and ecologically sound, with the main materials being bamboo, thatch and wood. Thick mud walls keep the heat in during cold winters, and make sure the house stays cool during hot summers.

SEPARATE ROOMS 👍

Even though the Meiteis have ancient traditions, they are quite modern when it comes to their homes. They believe that everyone must have their own room. So, a typical yumjao has separate rooms for all the people in the family.

SO SAFE

A lot of Manipur is earthquake-prone. That's why the houses are really light, so that even if they come crashing down due to an earthquake, no one will be hurt too badly. Brick and cement, on the other hand, are much heavier and more likely to cause injury.

Standing strong

I really am impressed by how creative the people of this state are. I bet they have some incredible monuments too!

That's a fact. You must remember that Manipur's history is very old, with many kings and wars. So there are a lot of forts, temples and palaces to be seen.

KANGLA FORT

This fort is very important, both historically and for religious reasons. It sits on the bank of the Imphal river in the city of Imphal. It was once the main seat of royalty. Two enormous dragon statues guard the entrance. An important temple devoted to Lord Koubru is also nearby, and local people come and pray here.

KANGLA PALACE

Since the earliest times, Kangla has been the place kings have chosen to live in. The Kangla Palace has been the royal residence since the first crowned king, Pakhangba. The palace is surrounded by a water body, sort of like a moat, called *kangla pat*.

SHREE GOVINDAJI TEMPLE

There are many followers of Lord Vishnu in Manipur, and this temple is the largest Vishnu temple in the state. It is in the heart of Imphal. Crowned by two gold-plated domes, the temple has images of Krishna (believed to be an avatar of Vishnu) and Radha. Many local people pray at this temple.

Govinda is yet another name for Lord Krishna.

A HISTORICAL VILLAGE

The village of Makhel takes you right back into history due to its many monuments that various tribes and kings stamped with their own cultural identity.

STORIES IN STONE

Makhel and its surrounding areas have many stones and artefacts that tell you a whole lot about how life was in those days. Tourists love to come and visit this little village.

A MENHIR MEMORIAL

The Naga tribes built this menhir, called *Tamarachu*, before they all went their own way.

A CENOTAPH

This cenotaph has three monoliths—two standing upright and one lying horizontal. According to tribal mythology, the cenotaph represents the animal kingdom, God and mankind. The Mao tribe believed that all three came from the same mother.

A cenotaph is a stone built in the memory of a person who may be buried elsewhere.

CROSSWORD TIME

Pushka is determined to solve this crossword in record time.
Can you help him out?

ACROSS

2. They guard the entrance to the Kangla Fort.

6. She is Krishna's beloved.

8. The holy place that Hindus worship at.

9. A god worshipped in Manipur.

10. The home of kings and queens.

DOWN

1. Another name for Lord Krishna.

2. Two of these crown the Shree Govindaji Temple.

3. The name of a fort and a palace too.

4. The channel of water that surrounds a fort.

5. A beloved god who has many names.

7. The capital of Manipur, where many kings lived.

A DEVIL'S HOME

Here's a cave to explore. The Khangkhui Mangsor Cave in Ukhrul is said to be one of India's earliest excavated caves. The cave is made of limestone. There is a huge hall in the centre, and legend has it that the devil king Mangsor used this as a meeting hall. There are many tunnels that take visitors to the chambers of the queens. Oh, yes! There was more than one queen.

A CAVE MAZE

The Tharon Cave or Thaeuluan Cave in Tamenglong is like a maze inside a cave. It's pitch dark inside. Cave expeditions, where visitors walk through the dark passages, are organized at regular intervals here. It is wise to follow a map, or you could easily get lost!

How exciting to explore a cave! Scary too!

THE MENHIR

The famous menhir at Imphal was built to demarcate a boundary. It was once a busy marketplace. It's said to be as old as the fifth century CE. There are some human figures carved on the menhir. People say these are probably the earliest folk carvings in Manipur.

There were some incredible menhirs and monolithic structures in ancient Europe that we can see even now like the Stonehenge.

A menhir is a standing stone, which usually holds some religious importance.

MENHIR SHADOW

Can you spot the exact shadow of these menhirs that Mishki has drawn?

A

B

C

D

E

A WAR MEMORIAL

The Khongjom War Memorial was built in memory of the brave soldiers who lost their lives in the war between the British and the Manipuri troops. Every year, on 23 April, people pay homage to the martyrs with gun salutes and prayers.

A FRIENDSHIP BRIDGE

The Indo-Myanmar Friendship Bridge, starting in the town of Moreh, is a 160-km highway bridge. It stretches across rivers and land, and links the two countries. It's not just a mark of friendship—it has also helped trade between India and Myanmar.

REMEMBERING PAST HEROES

Ningshing Khubham is a memorial to all the Manipuri heroes who have fought battles over the centuries. Also called the Ancestral Heroes Complex, there are statues of revered heroes like Paona Brajabashi, Bir Tikendrajit, Thangal General and Meitei Lai. On 13 August every year the people of Manipur celebrate Patriots' Day.

SHAHEED MINAR

This is a historic monument that commemorates and honours the people who fought for independence from the British and lost their lives doing so.

A BURIAL PLACE

Some years ago, archaeologists were very excited. They had found a place where they discovered many interesting facts about the way tribals had lived in ancient times. This was a place called Sekta, in Imphal, which had once been a burial place for tribes. Archaeologists found artefacts that told them a lot of about tribal rituals, customs and practices. Even now, history lovers visit this place to get a taste of the past.

JUMBLED UP

Pushka has got some names mixed up. Can you help him unjumble the words?

1. Sekta was a burial place for _____ **BITSER**.

2. Khongjom War Memorial is where people honour war _____ **EEHSRO**.

3. Shaheed _____ **IMARN** is a place where people remember martyrs.

4. On 13 _____ **GSTUUA**, Manipuris celebrate Patriots' Day.

5. The Friendship Bridge helps _____ **RATED** between India and Myanmar.

MAZE MANIA

Mishki and Pushka simply love mazes. And they love the monuments they have seen! Can you help them find their way out of the different mazes and reach all the monuments?

Working hard

Daadu, if it's mostly tribes who live in this state, farming must be the main occupation. Am I right?

You're right; there are many farmers in this state. But over the years, as towns and cities were built, industries were set up. And now there are many occupations that people are involved in.

Potato farm in Manipur

FARMER, FARMER, WHAT DO YOU GROW?

Farming is the most important activity in Manipur. Farmers grow rubber, tea, coffee, potatoes, oranges and cardamom. That's apart from the main crop—rice. There are some lush orchards too, where farmers grow pineapples, lemons, pears, peaches and so much more.

SHARING THE BURDEN

Manipuri women, who often help men in the fields, have a concept called *khutlang*, which means 'to lend a hand and get something in return'. Women collect in groups of ten and work in different fields. Often, instead of money, they get paid in kind. The system works well because everyone is happy this way.

TERRACE TRICK

With so much of the land on slopes, farmers have to carve terraces to make their fields. It's hard work, but they have to do it in order to grow the crops that only grow on flat land.

FRUIT SUDOKU

Can you help Mishki complete this fruit sudoku? You need to make sure that every row and column in each segment has one of each fruit.

ANIMAL FARM

Many tribes in these hills keep domestic animals. They don't necessarily do this as a business, but for their own use. Milk, eggs and meat are the main uses of such animals. Many tribes also live off the land, with fish as their staple food.

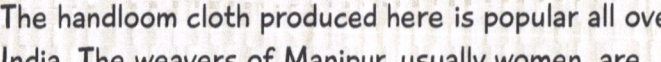
Silk-making factory in Manipur

SMALL INDUSTRIES

There are many people in Manipur who work in small industries that have been set up over the years. Sericulture (producing silk), soap-making, leather and carpentry are some.

WEAVING MAGIC

The handloom cloth produced here is popular all over India. The weavers of Manipur, usually women, are really talented and their work is wonderful. Also called *laichamphi*, this cloth they produce is turned into shawls, saris and used as drapes too!

Weaving is hard work. It can take weeks to make a single blanket.

CREATIVE CRAFTSMEN

The crafts of Manipur prove that the people here are truly talented. They work with a variety of materials—making dolls, crafting bamboo and cane baskets and furniture, carving wonderful designs into stone and hand-embroidering things. There are a lot of skills to choose from in this state.

Black pottery

Cane furniture

Time to sketch

Mishki can't weave a bamboo basket, but she has tried to draw one. Can you copy it and draw one yourself?

Draw here

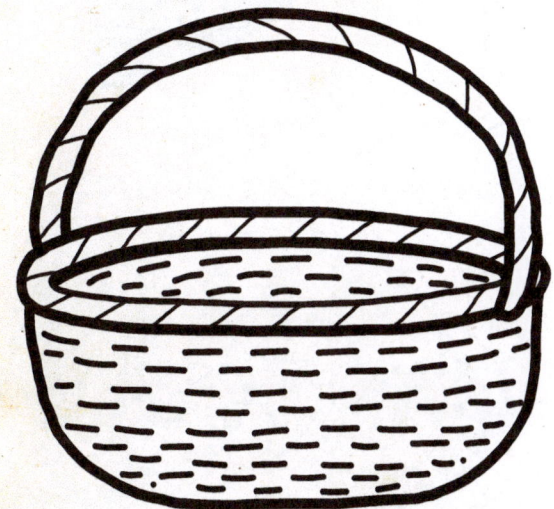

Yum yum yum

Yay! Time to eat. I can't wait, Daadu.

In that case, simply wash your hands and get set for some treats. Let's explore Manipuri cuisine.

HEALTHY TREATS

The one word that best describes Manipuri food is 'healthy'. Most dishes use little or no oil, so you can imagine how nutritious that makes the food. But it's spicy, all right! The staple food on most Manipuri tables is fish and vegetables.

NGARI—AN ACQUIRED TASTE

The people of Manipur love this dish. This is a kind of fish that is fermented and then cooked. It is used in a lot of dishes and is usually eaten with rice.

Woman selling dried fish

CHEERS FOR CHAMTHONG

Also called kangshoi, here's a super healthy dish. A lot of seasonal vegetables are chopped up, boiled and seasoned. It's a soup-like dish, which people love to have with rice.

MOROK METPA

This is an accompaniment to the main meal. A mix of chillies, onions and the ngari fish, this yummy salad-like dish adds zing to a meal, and people love to have it as a side dish.

EROMBA ENJOYMENT

Many of the Seven Sister states love this dish. It's a delicious mix of boiled vegetables and fish. Healthy? Of course!

45

SALAD DAYS

Singju is a yummy salad in which you can add just about any vegetable you can think of: onions, cabbage, lotus stem, ginger and anything else you want! People enjoy eating this as a snack as well as an accompaniment to a main meal.

TOMATO TRICK

Here's a truly unusual dessert. Fried tomatoes in sugar syrup! You heard that right. Khamen athoomba ashinba is a much-loved dessert in which tomatoes are fried and dunked in sugar syrup.

Looks really interesting, doesn't it?

SANA THONGBA

Here's an enormously popular dish. It's a Manipuri paneer curry. The paneer is dunked in a gravy that is made using milk. People eat it with great relish—especially during festivals.

JOYFUL DUMPLINGS

Madhurjan thongba is a dish that will make you smile. It's a yummy dessert made of gram flour dumplings soaked in milk. Pop one in your mouth, and you're bound to want another . . . and another . . . and another!

SWEET SOMETHING

Chahou kheer is the Manipuri version of the nationally popular kheer. It's a rice pudding made by cooking rice in milk and adding flavourful dry fruit. This is a real comfort food, and many grandparents make this for their grandchildren.

FOOD MATCH

Pushka can't stop eating. To distract him, Mishki has asked him to match the food to the right description. Can you help out?

Madhurjan thongba	A soup-like dish
Khamen athoomba ashinba	Gram flour dumplings
Singju	A paneer dish
Chamthong	A yummy salad
Sana thongba	A fried tomato dessert

What to wear?

Daadu, I simply love the clothes the people here wear. They are so creative and different. I'd love to try some Manipuri outfits.

If that's the case, you're in luck. You can try on some of the lovely clothing that people wear in Manipur. Come, let's see what these are.

DIFFERENT DRAPES

Though different tribes have slight differences in their attire, the clothing that women wear follows a similar trend. The main garment is called a *phanek*, which is like a sarong. Women drape it around their waists. A traditional phanek is striped. They also wear a shawl called an *innap*. During festivals or special occasions, women wear dresses called *chin phi* and *lai phi*. These are variations of the phanek skirt.

Even young girls today wear innaps. They simply team it up with a stylish blouse to keep their outfit modern!

Innap

Phanek

TRADITIONAL TRENDS

Typically, Manipuri men wear a dhoti with a kurta. They add on a jacket and a turban to complete the ensemble. When there is a ritual, men wear a special dhoti called a *khamen chatpa*. In the olden days, only certain people were allowed to wear one. But now it is a festive outfit worn by many.

Khamen chatpa

TRIBAL STYLES

Different tribes wear different types of clothing.

During the Ras Lila performance, dancers wear special costumes called *polois* and *kumins*.

SOMETHING'S ODD

Mishki is going to dress up. But there's one piece of clothing that's out of place in each row. Can you spot it?

| SARONG | DHOTI | INNAP | SHOES |

| SWEATER | SHAWL | CAP | MUFFLER |

| SCARF | HAT | SOCKS | CAP |

| SKIRT | INNAP | BELT | KILT |

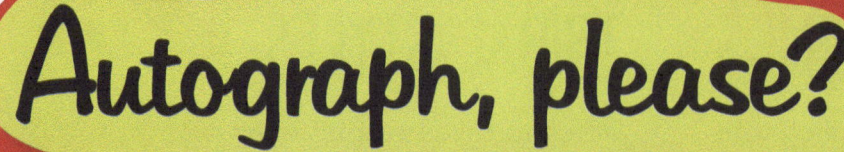

Autograph, please?

Are we going to meet some famous people now, Daadu?

Well, some of them are very famous, while some may not be as well known. But they have all done amazing things in their lives. It'll be an honour to get to know them.

DR THOUDAM DAMODARA SINGH

Known as His Holiness Bhaktisvarupa Damodara Swami Srila Sripada, this brilliant man brought together science and religion in an amazing way. He spoke to philosophers, scientists and saints from all over the world, and brought forth new ideas. He was a poet, educationist and singer too, and was an inspiration to people all over the world because of his ideas regarding religion and peace.

SANAKHYA EBOTOMBI HAAROKCHAM

This talented personality was a playwright, film director and writer who became quite an icon in Manipur. He started the Avant Garde Theatre Centre in Imphal, where many famous actors have been trained.

NAMEIRAKPAM KUNJARANI DEVI

This weightlifting champion has won the most medals among Indian sportswomen. She has set new national records and won several trophies at the national level.

CHUNGNEIJANG MARY KOM HMANGTE

Mary Kom has been nicknamed Magnificent Mary by adoring fans.

Better known as Mary Kom, this boxing champ has captured the imagination of thousands of young people. She became the first Indian female boxer to win a gold medal at the Asian Games. In fact, her accomplishments led to a popular biopic being made about her. Her grit and determination to succeed in a space where women rarely venture is legendary.

ASHANGBAM MINAKETAN SINGH

He is known as the founder of modern Meitei literature. He has authored many poems, essays, biographies and articles. Before he became a writer, he was a soldier in the Manipur Army. He fought fiercely against the British and was even jailed for several years.

IROM CHANU SHARMILA

Known as the Iron Lady, she is a strong-minded activist who went on a long hunger strike—more than fifteen years! She has been called the world's longest hunger striker. She was protesting against the ill-treatment of people in the north-eastern states, specifically against a law passed by the government that gave the army the authority to arrest and search people at will.

ARAMBAM  SUNITIKUMAR SINGH

A truly talented man, this artist took up his family's traditional art of woodcarving. He carved the most amazing scenes in wood, especially of simple people and the hardships they face. He won many national awards for his work and is now considered an important artist.

Arambam Sunitikumar Singh receiving an award

AMARJIT SINGH KIYAM ⚽

This youngster is a teen football idol. He has played many football matches for India. He was also a part of the Indian team for the 2017 FIFA Under-17 World Cup.

CELEBRITY MATCH

Can you match the name of the celebrity to what they are famous for? Pushka is sure he can do it!

Amarjit Singh Kiyam •	• **Wood artist**
Mary Kom •	• **Social activist**
Nameirakpam Kunjarani Devi •	• **Founder of Manipuri literature**
Irom Chanu Sharmila •	• **Weightlifting champ**
Arambam Sunitikumar Singh •	• **Boxer**
Ashangbam Minaketan Singh •	• **Footballer**

Yay! It's story time. What story are you going to tell us this time, Daadu?

I am going to tell you an amazing story that people have been telling their children for generations. The tribes here live amidst nature, and many of their stories are about animals.

THE TIGER, THE ELEPHANT AND THE FROG

In the deep, deep jungles of Manipur, there lived a fierce tiger and a strong elephant. Both beasts were convinced that he, and only he, should be recognized by all the other animals as the king of the jungle, and they would often taunt each other.

'You are nothing,' the tiger sneered one day. 'Have you heard me roar? I'm loud enough to shake the mountains.'

'Hah!' retorted the elephant. 'Have you seen how strong I am? I'm powerful enough to move the mountains.'

For several days the two animals circled each other, snarling, growling and trumpeting. The other animals shivered and shuddered. They didn't know what kind of violence these two beasts would unleash.

A wily fox decided to take matters into his own hands.

'Why don't you have a contest?' he suggested. 'We can have three rounds and whoever wins the contest will be recognized as the king of the jungle.'

The tiger and the elephant thought about this.

'This is a good idea,' grunted the tiger at last.

'Okay, I am ready for the contest,' harrumphed the elephant. 'But it's no contest. I will win hands down, you'll see.'

A day was chosen. All the animals gathered to watch the contest. The first round was a roaring round. The animals stuffed leaves and twigs into their ears. They could only imagine how loud it was going to be.

The elephant trumpeted loudly. A tree shook.

The tiger roared. The tree fell.

The elephant trumpeted again. A hill shook.

The tiger roared again. The hill crumbled.

Clearly, the tiger won the first round.

The two beasts continued the contest. They roared till the ground shook, they ripped trees from the earth, they ran up the

mountainside to see who could run faster. Finally, it was declared that the tiger was the winner.

'Now, as per our contest, I am the king. And not just that—as king I can choose which beast I want to eat next. And that is you,' the tiger panted. He was tired from the contest. 'First, I must drink some water. When I am back, I will eat you.'

The poor elephant had no option but to agree to this. After all, this was the rule of the jungle. He sat despondently, awaiting his fate.

Suddenly, he heard a croaking sound. He looked around in surprise.

Croak, croak! It was a little frog. 'Would you like my help? I can make sure you are crowned the king of the jungle, but if I do, I want certain privileges.'

'You?' scoffed the elephant. 'How can a mere frog help a giant like me?'

'Wait and see,' the frog said with a grin.

Just then, the tiger came back, licking his lips. He was looking forward to a hearty meal. But he stopped when he saw the frog.

'I have come to challenge you,' the frog said.

'Ha! You? Challenge me?' the tiger sneered.

'I can race you to the edge of the mountain,' the frog said. 'And if I win, the elephant will be king.'

The tiger found this so funny that he agreed at once.

The race began. Unknown to the tiger, the frog had jumped on to the tiger's back. When they reached the edge of the mountain, the frog leapt off and landed in front of the tiger.

The tiger was stunned to see the frog ahead of him. He hung his head in shame. He had to agree to abide by the terms of this new contest and accept the elephant as king.

This is why some tribes in the jungles of Manipur believe that the elephant is the king of the jungle.

TRAVEL DIARY

Have you enjoyed this trip to Manipur with your friends Mishki and Pushka—and, of course, with Daadu Dolma?

Now you can make your own Manipur diary. And if you ever visit Manipur, make sure you take pictures and put them in the photo box.

The first place I would visit in Manipur:

_____

I think the most interesting historical figure from Manipur is:

_____

The one dish I am definitely going to eat:

_____

The monument I think is the most interesting:

_____

The one famous person from Manipur I would love to meet:

_____

If I were from Manipur, I would do this dance:

_____

The festival from Manipur that I think is the most fun:

_____

The five words that I think describe Manipur the best are:

_____

_____

_____

_____

_____

My Manipur memories:

ANSWERS

page 9 HIDDEN WORDS

Here are some of the words that can be formed: den, doe, don, end, eon, hen, her, nod, odd, one, ore, red, rod, roe, done, door, herd, hero, hood, horn, neon, nerd, none

page 13 SPOT THE DIFFERENCES

page 15 RHYME TIME

Czar, Rajah, Monarch, Ruler, Sovereign

page 17 CRACK THE CODE

HISTORY IS FASCINATING

page 19 WHAT'S ODD?

STUDENT, TEACHERS, PRIESTS

page 21 WORD MATCH

I love Manipur—Ei Manipur nungshi; Goodbye—Chatcharage; Hello—Khurumjari; Congratulations—Thakatchari; Please—Chaanbeeduna

page 27 WORD SEARCH

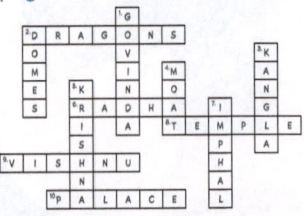

page 33 CROSSWORD TIME

page 35 MENHIR SHADOW

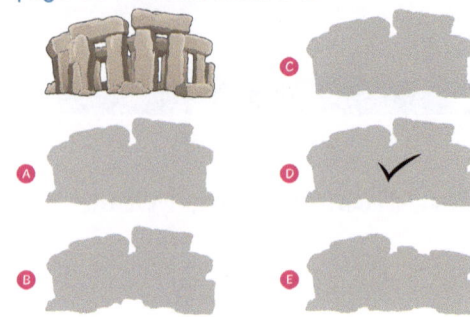

page 37 JUMBLED UP

TRIBES, HEROES, MINAR, AUGUST, TRADE

page 38-39 MAZE MANIA

page 41 FRUIT SUDOKU

page 47 FOOD MATCH

Madhurjan thongba—Gram flour dumplings; Khamen athoomba ashinba— A fried tomato dessert; Singju—A yummy salad; Chamthong—A soup-like dish; Sana thongba—A paneer dish

page 49 SOMETHINGS'S ODD

SHOES, CAP, SOCKS, BELT

page 53 CELEBRITY MATCH

Amarjit Singh Kiyam—Footballer; Mary Kom—Boxer; Nameirakpam Kunjarani Devi—Weightlifting champ; Irom Chanu Sharmila—Social activist; Arambam Sunitikumar Singh—Wood artist; Ashangbam Minaketan Singh—Founder of Manipuri literature